Let Us Believe in the
Beginning of the Cold Season

Forough Farrokhzad in Darband, Iran, July 5, 1956
Photograph by Sohrab Sepehri

Let Us Believe in the Beginning of the Cold Season

SELECTED POEMS

Forough Farrokhzad

*Translated from the Persian
by Elizabeth T. Gray, Jr.*

A New Directions Paperbook Original

FOR IRAJ, WHO KNEW HER.
THANK YOU.

*

New Directions thanks Kayhan London, Nazenin Ansar, Firoozeh (Ramezanzade), and Diana Ghooghasian for their assistance with the frontispiece photograph.

Manufactured in the United States of America
First published as a New Directions Paperbook (NDP1530) in 2022

Library of Congress Cataloging-in-Publication Data
Names: Farrukhzād, Furūgh, author. | Gray, Elizabeth T. Jr., translator.
Title: Let us believe in the beginning of the cold season : selected poems / Forough Farrokhzad ; translated from the Persian by Elizabeth T. Gray, Jr.
Other titles: Let us believe in the beginning of the cold season (Compilation)
Description: New York, NY : New Directions Paperbook Original, 2022.
Identifiers: LCCN 2021047417 | ISBN 9780811231657 (paperback)
Subjects: LCSH: Farrukhzād, Furūgh—Translations into English.
Classification: LCC PK6561.F264 L48 2022 | DDC 891/.5513—dc23/eng/20211020
LC record available at https://lccn.loc.gov/2021047417

10 9 8 7 6 5

New Directions Books are published for James Laughlin
by New Directions Publishing Corporation
80 Eighth Avenue, New York 10011

ndbooks.com

Contents

Note on Transliteration

The Persian language is written using the Arabic alphabet. After reviewing scholarly approaches and consulting translators whom I admire, I have chosen a streamlined transliteration system based on pronunciation rather than orthography. Thus, I have used *s* for the letters *s, th,* and *zh; z* for both *z* and *dh.* Both *q* and *gh* are transliterated as *gh*, except where a proper noun is fixed in English, e.g. Qaf instead of Ghāf. I have also not transliterated established names, e.g. Farrokhzad, Reza Shah Pahlavi, Ferdowsi. Long vowels are marked as such with a diacritical line above the vowel. The ezāfeh, an unstressed sound linking words together, is transliterated as *-e*, to distinguish it from the letter *heh.* I have dropped the *v* where it is silent and follows *kh*; I have treated *yeh* inconsistently in several places to track pronunciation more closely.

Translator's Introduction

In a country where for centuries women have lived silenced, diminished, and in the shadow of their men, Forough ol-Zaman Farrokhzad (1934–1967) broke all the rules. In her life, in her poetry and film, and at high cost, she claimed space and voice. The best of her work can stand with any poem written by any poet in any culture at any time. She remains a beacon to artists, especially women and marginalized artists, who seek freedom in all its forms.

In the decades since her untimely death, biographical and critical essays, fictional accounts of her life, and translations of her work have appeared in numerous anthologies and dedicated volumes. This introduction offers a brief sketch of her life and places these translations within the broader context of her legacy.

*

The third of seven children, Farrokhzad was born on December 29, 1934, in Mazandaran, north of Tehran. At the time, Iran was undergoing accelerated and wrenching modernization under the rule of Reza Shah Pahlavi, the Army general who deposed the last Qajar monarch in 1925. A few years later Farrokhzad's family moved to a middle-class neighborhood in Tehran. Unlike many of his peers, her father, career military officer Colonel Mohammad Bāgher Farrokhzad, ensured that all of his children had access to education and to the histories and classical literature in his library. His four sons went to German universities; two of his daughters became part of the Iranian intelligentsia. His wife, Tūrān, was pious and strict.

Farrokhzad attended a local co-educational elementary school until she was thirteen, during which time Reza Shah was exiled and Iran was occupied by British and Russian troops for the duration of World War II. At her all-girls secondary school she demonstrated an interest in literature and began to write poetry. At fifteen she left high school for a technical school where she studied painting and dressmaking. Bold and rebellious, her independent streak presented a challenge to every kind of parental control. At sixteen she became entranced with a distant cousin, Parvīz Shāpūr, a journalist and satirist who worked at the Ministry of

Finance. He was eleven years her elder, and both sets of parents disapproved of the match. Nonetheless, Farrokhzad insisted on marrying him, and they relented. In 1952 she moved with Shāpūr to Ahvāz in southwestern Iran. Ahvāz was provincial, her mother-in-law overbearing, and within the year Farrokhzad had given birth to her only child, a son, Kāmyār, whom she adored. She felt claustrophobic, isolated, and bored. She poured herself into her poems and began to submit them to literary journals in Tehran.

From the outset, the content and point of view in her poems were deemed sensational. While for centuries Persian poetry had explored the nuances of love—lover, Beloved, love lost, love longed-for, human or divine—the poetic speaker had rarely been a woman, and certainly not a flesh- and-blood passionate woman speaking from her heart, a speaker easily identified with the author. Shāpūr encouraged her work and tolerated her solo travel to Tehran to meet with editors. His parents, and hers, believed that married women who treasured their reputation, and the honor of their husbands and households, didn't do such things. Rumors of liaisons with men in Tehran began to circulate. The title poem of her first collection, "Captive," written by the nineteen-year-old Farrokhzad in 1954, speaks to her feelings of imprisonment, longing, and despair.

Farrokhzad and Shāpūr separated in the summer of 1955, just as *Captive (Asīr)* appeared and details of Farrokhzad's affair with Nāsser Khodāyār, editor of the literary journal *Rowshanfekr* ("enlightened, open-thinking, intelligentsia") began to emerge. Khodāyār had published "Sin," the opening poem of her next collection, a scorching and unrepentant first-person account of intimate sex. He also published, once their brief affair had ended, a thinly fictionalized account of their relationship in a major magazine. Scandal ensued. Name recognition was no longer a problem. Her divorce became final, requiring that she relinquish legal access to her son. Farrokhzad was free. She had changed Persian poetry. But the combined pressures of loss, isolation, and critical attacks were overwhelming. In the fall of 1955 she had a nervous breakdown and spent a month in the Rezā'ī psychiatric clinic, where she underwent electroshock therapy.

In mid-1956, as her second collection *Wall (Dīvār)* started to circulate, Farrokhzad left Iran and spent fourteen months in Rome and Germany. While abroad, her encounters with European artists working in theater, film, and innovative literary forms had an enormous impact on her work. "From Far Away," "Knot," and "Much Later" were written in Munich, and would appear in her next collection, *Rebellion* (*Osyān*).

Upon returning to Tehran in the fall of 1957 she went to work for *Ferdowsi*, an important literary magazine in Tehran, and moved in the city's circle of writers and intellectuals. In 1958, when *Rebellion* appeared, she applied for a job at the film studio of Ebrahīm Golestān, a brilliant and broadly educated writer and filmmaker. Although he was married, and remained so, they began a deep and enduring relationship that, despite vicious gossip and criticism, lasted until her death. She studied film in England briefly in 1959, and edited a number of documentaries before directing, in 1962, *The House is Black*, a short documentary filmed at a leper colony in northwestern Iran. The film is acknowledged to be a forerunner of the New Wave cinema in Iran, and won the prize for Best Documentary at the Oberhausen Short Film Festival in 1963. Critics felt the film spoke, obliquely, to the political environment in the country.

That political environment was becoming increasingly hostile to intellectuals. After the American-and British-backed coup toppled nationalist Prime Minister Mohammad Mossadegh in 1953, Shah Mohammad Reza Pahlavi, while continuing to push modernization, became increasingly intolerant of dissent. Activists, artists, and writers, and the institutions that supported them, were suppressed or punished. In the summer of 1963 in the holy city of Qom, clerical resistance to the Shah's reforms erupted in riots that were brutally crushed.

Another Birth (*Tavallodī Dīgar*), Farrokhzad's fourth collection, was published in 1964. She saw it as a turning point, its perspective broader than the strictly personal frame of her earlier work. Longing and loss are still present, but the speaker's perspective has moved past innocence, informed by bleak experience. "Those Days" looks back at the lost delights of childhood; "Earthly Verses" paints an apocalyptic world that has lost light and faith; "Wind-Up Doll" eviscerates the way in which women are treated in Iranian culture; "O Jeweled Land" mocks everything the new society has become; "The Victory of the Garden" celebrates the natural world that protects the happy, renegade lovers from the world's opprobrium. These poems are sonically rich, and use syntax, lexical variation, lineation, and repetition in powerful ways; they are clearly the work of a writer in full control of all aspects of her poetic art. The collection was widely acknowledged as ground-breaking, and solidified Farrokhzad's stature as a major poet.

Between 1964 and 1967 she continued to work in film, to act, to travel, and to write. In February of 1967 she died in a car accident. Her final collection of poems, *Let Us Believe in the Beginning of the Cold Season* (*Īmān Biāvarīm Beh Āghāz-e Fasl-e Sard*), was published in 1974.

*

I began to study Persian in the 1970s, in Iran and in the U.S., solely to read and translate Hafez, the most revered poet in the language. Iran's classical poets were my gateway into its literature. In 2013, *Mantis,* a literary journal at Stanford University, offered me as much space as I needed for a translation of a contemporary Persian poet. I chose "Let Us Believe in the Beginning of the Cold Season," largely because I had long been drawn to its baffling title. It is Farrokzhad's longest poem, originally published in the fall of 1965 in *Ārash*, a literary magazine in Tehran. Working through the poem required the better part of a year and consultations with friends, scholars, and other translators. The poem stunned me with its precision, its devastating imagery, its terrifying blend of wisdom, hope, and grief. It is, in my view, a masterpiece, written by a poet at the height of her powers. The recursive imagery and music, the stark vision, the allusive range, the unerring control over syntax and lineation—this was what poetry could be, what it could offer in, and in spite of, a dark time. It is a poem at once excruciatingly introspective, yet overwhelmingly universal in its reach. When New Directions asked if I would consider translating a selection of her work, I eagerly agreed.

This edition includes the poems of Farrokhzad I admire most, the ones that "talk with me," to steal a phrase from an exchange with Dr. Farzaneh Milani, the preeminent scholar of Farrokhzad and her work. They include poems from all of her books, with most of them drawn from her middle to late work. Her posthumous volume, *Let Us Believe in the Beginning of the Cold Season*, is included in its entirety. I've also added brief contextual notes to the poems in the back of the book, as well as a selected bibliography for further reading.

I have found no critical edition of Farrokhzad's poetry. I have worked from a text published in Sweden, clearly offset from a Persian original, that contains blank spaces where government censors had redacted segments of poems. I have filled in missing lines from other editions of her work. This lack of a critical edition exacerbates formatting problems: stanza breaks and punctuation vary, sometimes dramatically, from one version to another. Compounding the problem is the fact that Persian orthography does not distinguish uppercase from lowercase letters. Translators have had broad license to format her work in a target language.

I have assumed that Farrokhzad made deliberate lyric choices that need no clarification or correction, and that the Swedish text assembled work she had reviewed and approved prior to her death. I have tried to adhere to the original text as it appears on the page, with its ambiguities. That said, I have inserted the occasional internal comma and have capitalized words that most clearly begin a sentence.

Every translation reflects an intense engagement with, and a close reading of, something ineffable even in its original language. Each translation of Farrokhzad reflects a translator's encounter with her work, and how they have been changed by it. I am always after what the poet actually wrote, the specific words on the page, trying to craft an English version that captures as much of the beauty, strangeness, ferocity, and stillness of the original as possible. In preparing this selection, I have benefited from the wisdom of my colleague Iraj Anvar, who moved in the same avant-garde circles in Tehran and knew Farrokhzad when she was in Rome. I have also had access to the work of Farrokhzad scholars and that of her many English translators. These encounters have been deeply informative and I am grateful for their work.

Let Us Believe in the
Beginning of the Cold Season

Captive

اسیر   *Asīr*

I want you, and I know that never
will I hold you as my heart desires
You are that clear bright sky
I am a captive bird in the corner of this cage

From behind the cold dark bars
my longing look is astonished at your face
I think that a hand might appear
and suddenly free me to fly to you

I think that in a moment of carelessness
I might fly from this silent prison
I might laugh in the face of the jailor
I might begin to live again, at your side

I am thinking and I know that never
will I have the resolve to leave this cage
Even if it were the jailor's wish
I have no strength left for flight

From beyond the bars each bright morning
a child's gaze smiles in my face
When I begin a joyous song
his lips come to me with a kiss

O sky, if I wish one day
to fly from this silent prison
what will I say to the eyes of the crying child?
Leave me be, I am a captive bird

I am the candle whose burning heart
lights up a ruin
If I choose silence
I will shred a nest

Sin

گناه *Gonāh*

I sinned a sin full of pleasure
in an embrace that was warm and fiery
I sinned in arms that were hot
and vindictive and made of iron

In that dark and silent sanctuary
I looked into his eyes full of secrets
My restless heart trembled in my chest
at the demands of his hungry eyes

In that dark and silent sanctuary
I sat agitated at his side
His lips poured violent desire across my lips
I was freed from my mad heart's grief

I whispered words of love into his ear:
I want you, O my love
I want you, O life-giving embrace
You, O my mad lover

The passion in his eyes lit a flame
Red wine danced in the cup
In the soft bed my euphoric body
trembled on his chest

I sinned a sin full of pleasure
beside a dazed and trembling body
O Lord, what do I know about what I did
in that dark and silent sanctuary

Lost

گمشده   *Gomshodeh*

O, after those insanities
I don't believe I'm sane
It's as if *she* has died in me, I'm so
exhausted and silent and erased

Dejected, every moment I ask the mirror
What is left of me, what do you see?
But—no, no—in the mirror I see
that I'm not even a shadow of what I was

Coquettishly, like that Hindu dancer
I stamp my foot—but on my grave
Look how, with a hundred regrets
I have lit up this ruin with my light

I do not seek the road to the city of day
Doubtless I am lying at the bottom of a grave
I have a jewel, but out of fear
I have hidden it in the heart of the swamps

I am walking . . . but I do not ask myself
Where is the road . . . ? Where is home . . . ? What is the goal?
I give kisses but I don't know who it is
this mad heart worships

When *she* died in me everything that was
suddenly looked different to me
as if night with its two cold hands
embraced my restless soul

Ah ... yes ... this is me.... but what's the use
Now *she* who was in me is no longer, is no longer
I roar madly under my breath
She who was in me, who was she, who was she?

Grief-Worshipper

اندوه پرست *Andūh-parast*

I wish I were like autumn. . . . I wish I were like autumn
I wish I were, like autumn, silent and depressing
The leaves of my desires would turn yellow one by one
The sun of my eyes would grow cold
The sky of my heart would be full of pain
Suddenly a storm of grief would clutch my soul
Like rain my tears would stain my skirt
Oh . . . how beautiful it would be if I were autumn
I would be wild and passionate and colorful
In my eyes a poet would read . . . a heavenly poem
Beside me in the embers of a painful hidden fire
the lover's heart would flare
My song . . .
Like the voice of the broken-winged wind
grief's perfume would pour over wounded hearts
Before me:
the bitter face of youth's winter
Behind me:
the tumult of a summer of sudden love
Inside me:
the home of grief and pain and suspicion
I wish I were like autumn. . . . I wish I were like autumn

Wall

ديوار   *Dīvār*

In the hurried passing of cold moments
your savage eyes, in their silence
build a wall around me
I flee from you down an unmarked road
so that I may see the fields in moon dust
so that I may wash my body in springs of light
so that in the colorful mist of a warm summer morning
I may fill my skirt with wild lilies
so that I may hear the call of the roosters from the roof of a peasant's hut

I flee from you
so that in the embrace of the wilderness
I may press my foot firmly on its greenness
or drink the grasses' cold dew

I flee from you so that on an abandoned beach
from above rocks lost in a cloud of darkness
I may see the dizzy dance of the sea's storms

Like wild pigeons
in a faraway sunset, I would take under my wing
the plains, the mountains, the skies
so that I might hear from the folds of dry bushes
the happy melodies of wild birds

I flee from you so that, far from you, I may open
the road to the city of desires
and within the city . . .
the heavy gold lock on the palace of dreams

But with their silent roar your eyes
blur my view of every road in sight
while the darkness of their secret
builds a wall around me

Finally, one day . . .
I will flee from the spellbinding eyes of doubt
I will rise like scent from colorful dream-flowers
I will crawl in the waves of the night wind's hair
I will go to the shore of the sun

In a world sleeping in eternal peace
I will slide gently into the bed of gold-colored clouds
Rays of light will cast melodies
across the face of the joyful sky

From there, happy and free
I will see a world whose roads
your spellbinding eyes have blurred
I will see a world around which
your spellbinding eyes
in the darkness of their secret
have built a wall

God's Rebellion

عصیان خدا   *Osyān-e Khodā*

If I were God one night I would order the angels
to drop the sun's disk into the furnace of darkness
In anger, I would order the caretakers of the universe
to pick the moon's yellow leaf from the branch of night

At midnight, behind the veils of my grand palace
the hand of my roaring rage would turn the world upside down
After thousands of years of silence my tired hands
would cast down the mountains into the open mouth of the sea

I would unchain the feet of thousands of feverish stars
I would scatter the fire's blood in the silent veins of the forests
I would tear the veils of smoke so that in the wind's roar
the daughter of fire may dance drunk in the depth of the forests

On a flute I would blow a spell like the night wind
so that the rivers, tired of a life sluicing wet channels
would rise from their beds like thirsty snakes and pour down
into the heart of the night sky's dull marsh

Softly I would tell the winds to launch, on the river of feverish night
the small skiff drunk on the roses' perfume
I would open the graves so that thousands of wandering souls
could once again conceal themselves inside bodies

If I were God, one night I would order the angels
to boil the water of Heaven's river in the furnace of Hell
and, burning torch in hand, to drive the flock of pious ones
out of the green debauched pasture of Heaven

Weary of zealous restraint, at midnight, in Satan's bed
I would seek shelter in the descent to a fresh sin
I would choose instead of the golden crown of divinity
the dark and painful pleasure of sin's embrace

Knot

گره‎ *Gereh*

If tomorrow hadn't arrived
I would have stayed by your side forever
I would have sung the song of my love forever
in the sunlight of your love

Beyond the windows of your room
that night had a cold black stare
In the darkness the tunnel of your eyes
led into the depths of your soul

The image of us, broken and motionless
slid downward in the dusty mirror
Your hair was the color of wheat stalks
my hair, wavy and pitch-black

A secret burned in my heart
I wanted to speak with you
but a knot cut off my voice
In the shade, under a bush, nothing grows!

From there my tired gaze flew off
and spun erratically around my body
Inside the golden frame
the eyes of the Messiah laughed at my pain

I saw the room confused, in disarray
your book fallen at my feet
my hairpins fallen
there on your bed

No more sound of bubbling water
from the fish tank
What worries
kept your old cat awake?

Mute and tired my agitated gaze
turned back toward you again
I wanted it to speak to you
but facing you it was silent

Then white stars of tears
twinkled in the night of my eyelashes
I saw your hands like a cloud
come toward my astonished face

I saw the warm wing of your breath
brush against my cold neck
as if a lost breeze rustled
in the wild thickets of my pain

A hand poured the lead of silence
and the grain of quiet into my heart
I was tired of this painful struggle
I headed for the city of oblivion

I forgot the grief of tomorrow
I said: "Journey" was a bitter fairytale
Suddenly that perfumed golden moment
spread over my life

That night I drank happy songs
from your lips
That night your kiss scattered the drop of eternity
into the mouth of my love

Return

بازگشت *Bāzgasht*

At last the ribbon of road ended
I arrived covered with dust
My gaze rushed ahead of me
On my lips a warm "Hello"

The town boiled in the pot of noon
The alleyway burned in the fever of the sun
Across the silent pavement my feet
moved forward, trembling

The houses had changed color
dust-covered, dark, depressing
Faces encased in chadors
like ghosts in shackles

Like a blind eye the dried-up gutters
empty of water and any trace of him
A man passed by singing
My ears filled with his song

The familiar dome of the old mosque
looked like a broken bowl
From the minaret a believer chanted
the call to prayer with a sad voice

Barefoot children ran after dogs
stones in hand
A woman laughed from behind her veil
The wind snapped a shutter shut

From the dark mouths of entryways
came the damp scent of graves
A blind man tapping his cane passed by
An acquaintance approached from a distance

A door opened silently there
Hands pulled me toward themselves
A tear rained down from the cloud of eyes
Hands pushed me away from themselves

Again the old ivy on the face of the wall
rippled like a trembling stream
the dense thick leaves an ancient green
dulled by the dust of time

My gaze, searching, asked:
"Where is there still a trace of him?"
but I saw my little room
was empty of his childish voice

Suddenly, from the heart of the mirror's cold soil
his image sprouted up like a flower
His velvet eyes washed over me
Ah, in his imagination he saw me too!

I leaned against the wall
Softly I said: "Is this you, Kāmī?"
but I saw that from that bitter past
nothing is left but a name

At last the ribbon of road ended
I arrived covered with dust
The road didn't lead the thirsty to the spring
My town was the grave of my desires

From Far Away

از راهی دور   *Az Rāhi Dūr*

I look off toward your town and into your palm
No further message or sign of you
On the road no ray of hope's moonlight
In the heart no shadow of a hidden secret

The desert is scorched, without the fine drops
of the spring rain's kiss
In night's expanse no hoofbeats of horsemen
on the invisible road

You are one with her only in that moment
when she is lost to herself in your embrace
When you open the ring of your arms
I know well she's been forgotten

Who draws you in, with her sparkling eyes
and burning lips, at the bend of the road?
Or in that magical silent sanctuary
where her hand has kindled the lantern of sin?

You never gave me your heart, although
my thirst had scalded your body like fire
I who had learned the art of sorcery
in the legendary school of Zohreh

Like a shoreline I opened my embrace to you
My heart's desire was to be your beloved
"How could I not have known from the outset"
"There would come a day when I vexed your heart"

After this I'll want nothing from you
no greeting, no message, no sign
I'll go my own way and let you go yours
You're not the same, no longer what you were

Much Later

بعدها   *Ba'd-hā*

One day my death will come:
in a spring bright and awash in light
a long winter thick with fog
or an autumn empty of cries and ardor

One day my death will come:
one of those bittersweet days
an empty day like all other days
a shadow of todays, of yesterdays!

My eyes like dim passageways
my cheeks like cold marble
Suddenly sleep will seize me
I'll pass beyond screams of pain

Freed from poetry's spell, slowly my fingers
will trace the face of my notebook
I'll remember that the blood of poetry
once blazed in my hands

Every moment the soil will call me to itself
People will arrive to bury me
Ah, maybe at midnight my lovers
will place a flower on my sad grave

After me the dark veils of my world
will suddenly pull away from me
Unfamiliar eyes will pry into
my papers and notebooks

After me a stranger who remembers me
will enter my little room
Beside the mirror there is still
a strand of hair, a handprint, a comb

I'll be free of myself and stand apart from myself
Whatever is left will be ruin
Like a boat's sail my soul
will grow distant and hidden on the horizon

Days and weeks and months
will all impatiently hurry off
Waiting for a letter your eyes
will stare into the eyes of the roads

But then the clinging soil of the tomb
will press on my cold body
Without you, far from the beating of your heart
my heart will rot there under the soil

Much later rain and wind will gently wash away
my name from the face of my headstone
By the side of the road my grave will remain
nameless, free of the stories about me

Those Days

آن روزها   *Ān Rūz-hā*

Those days have gone
Those good days
Those wholesome overflowing days
Those skies full of sequins
Those branches laden with cherries
Those houses supporting one another inside the green protection of
   the ivy
Those rooftops of playful kites
Those alleyways dizzy from the perfume of the acacias

Those days have gone
Those days when my songs bubbled
from between my eyelids
My eyes drank in everything they touched
like fresh milk, as if they held
a restless happy hare
Each dawn, with the ancient sun
he went exploring in unfamiliar fields
Nights he sank into the forests of darkness

Those days have gone
Those snowy silent days
when from behind the window glass, in the warm room
every time I looked out
my pure snow fell gently
like soft fluff
on the worn-out wooden ladder
on the weak clothesline
on the tresses of the old pines
and I thought of tomorrow, ah
tomorrow . . .
a mass of slippery white

It began with the rustle of grandmother's chador
with her vague shadow in the doorway—
that suddenly freed itself in the cold sensation of light—
and with the erratic flight path of the pigeons
through the panes of stained glass
Tomorrow . . .

The warmth of the korsī brought sleep
Out of my mother's sight
I erased, quickly and fearlessly
checkmarks from my old exercise books
When the snow stopped
I wandered dejected in the garden
At the base of the pots of withered jasmine
I buried my dead sparrows

◊ ◊

Those days have gone
Those days of rapture and wonder
Those days of sleep and waking
Those days when every shadow held a secret
every closed box hid a treasure
In the noon silence the corner of every closet
seemed a world
In my eyes everyone unafraid of the dark
was a hero

Those days have gone
Those days of Nowruz
That waiting for the sun and the flowers
That frisson from the perfume
in the quiet and modest gathering of the wild narcissus that came
    to town
on the last morning of winter
Those voices of the peddlers in the long street with its patches of green

The bazaar floated in wandering smells
in the scent of coffee and fish
The bazaar widened underfoot, stretched out, blended with every
    moment of the way
and spun in the depths of dolls' eyes
The bazaar was Mother who sped toward the colored mass of the torrent
and came back
with boxes of gifts, with full baskets
The bazaar was rain that poured, that poured, that poured

◊ ◊

Those days have gone
Those days staring into the secrets of the flesh
Those days of cautious encounters with the beauty of blue-colored veins
on the hand that with a single flower
called out from behind the wall
to another hand
to an anxious, fearful, ink-stained, trembling hand
and love
with a shy hello revealed itself

In the hot smoky noons
we sang our love in the dust of the alleyway
We were acquainted with the simple language of dandelions
We took our hearts to the garden of innocent affections
and loaned them to the trees
and the ball carried kisses back and forth between our hands
and it was love, its sensual confusion
that in the darkness of the entryway
suddenly
surrounded us
and created the attraction between us, in hot thick breaths and
    pounding hearts and furtive smiles

◊ ◊

Those days have gone
Those days, like vegetation that rots in the sun
rotted from the sun's heat
and those alleyways dizzy with the perfume of the acacias were lost
in the mobbed uproar of the streets with no way back
and the girl who colored her cheeks
with the petals of geraniums, ah
now she is a woman alone
Now she is a woman alone

The Sun Comes Out

آفتاب میشود   *Āftāb Mīshavad*

Look at the grief inside my eyes
how it melts drop by drop
how my dark unruly shadow
settles in the sun's hands
Look
all of my existence crumbles

A spark devours me
It carries me to the zenith
It traps me
Look
all of my sky
fills with shooting stars

◊ ◊

You came from far, far away
from the land of perfumes and lights
Now you have seated me in a boat
of ivory, of cloud, of crystal
Take me, my lovely hope
Take me to the city of poems and passions

You drag me to the road filled with stars
You seat me higher than the stars
Look
I was scorched by the stars
I became brimful with fever stars
Like the red-colored fish
I nibbled at stars in the pools of night

Before this, how far away our world was
from these blue balconies of the sky
Now your voice
reaches my ear again
the sound of angels' snowy wings
Look at how far I've come
to the Milky Way, to the infinite, to the eternal

Now that we have reached the zeniths
wash me with the wine of the waves
wrap me in the silk of your kisses
want me in the slow-paced nights
Don't ever let me go
Don't separate me from these stars

◊ ◊

On our road look how the wax of night
melts drop by drop
To your warm lullaby
the black goblet of my eyes
becomes brimful with the wine of sleep
In the cradles of my poetry
look
you rise and the sun comes out

On the Soil

روى خاک   *Rū-ye Khāk*

I have never longed
to be a star in the mirage of the sky
or like the souls of the chosen
to be the silent companion of angels
Never have I been separate from the earth
I have not been acquainted with the stars
I am standing on the soil
with my body that, like the stem of a plant
is sucking in air and sun and water
in order to live

Pregnant with despair
Pregnant with pain
I am standing on the soil
so that the stars may praise me
so that the winds may caress me

◊ ◊

I peer out my little window
I am nothing but the echo of a song
I am not immortal
I seek nothing but the echo of a song
in moans of pleasure that are more pure
than the simple silence of sorrow
I do not seek to nest
in a body that is
as dew is on the iris of my body

◊ ◊

Life is my hut. On its walls
passers-by have drawn mementos
with the black line of love:
the arrow-pierced heart
the upside-down candle
the pale silent dots
on the mixed-up letters of madness

In my night that rested
on the surface of the river of memories
every lip that touched my lips
conceived a star
So why should I long for a star?

◊ ◊

This is my song
—soothing, pleasing
Before this, nothing more than this

The Wind Will Carry Us

باد ما را خواهد برد   *Bād Mā Rā Khāhad Bord*

Alas, in my little night
the wind has a tryst with the leaves of the trees
In my little night, there is the dread of devastation

Listen
Do you hear the gusts of darkness?
Excluded, I watch this happiness
I am addicted to my despair
Listen
Do you hear the gusts of darkness?

In the night, something is happening now
The moon is red and agitated
and above this roof that fears it will crumble at any moment
clouds like a crowd of mourners
wait for the moment to rain

A moment
then nothing
Beyond this window night shudders
and the Earth
ceases to spin
Beyond this window an unknown
is watching you and me

O you, green from head to toe
put your hands like a burning memory in my lovestruck hands
and entrust your lips like a warm feeling of existence
to the caresses of my lovestruck lips
The wind will carry us with it
The wind will carry us with it

In the Green Waters of Summer

در آبهای سبز تابستان   *Dar Āb-hā-ye Sabz-e Tābestān*

Lonelier than a leaf
with my weight of vanished joys
in the green waters of summer
I sail peacefully
toward the realm of death
toward the shore of autumn griefs

I abandoned myself in a shadow
in the untrustworthy shadow of love
in the fleeting shadow of happiness
in the shadow of what cannot last

Nights when a dizzy breeze whirls
in the low sad sky
Nights when a bloody mist collects
in the blue alleyways of our veins
Nights when
my lonely loneliness—
with the trembling of our souls—
gushes in every pulse-beat
the feeling of life, sick life

"In the waiting of the valleys is a secret"
They carved this onto the face of the mountains
on the mighty rocks
Those who fell one night
filled the mountains' silence
with a bitter plea

"In the agitation of full hands
there is not the peace of empty ones.
The silence of ruins is beautiful."

This a woman sang in the waters
in the green waters of summer
as if she lived among ruins

With our breaths
we contaminate one another
Contaminated by the virtue of happiness
in the gardens of our kisses
we fear the sound of the wind
we pale at the influence of suspicion's shadows
At every feast in the palace of light
we shudder, afraid it will crumble

◊ ◊

Now you are here
spread out like the perfume of the acacias
in the morning's alleyways
heavy on my chest
hot in my hands
lost in my hair, immolated, unconscious
Now you are here

Something vast and dark and thick
something disturbed like the sounds of far-off days
whirls and spreads itself
across my agitated pupils

Maybe they pull me from the cool spring
Maybe they pick me from the branch
Maybe they close me like a door to what comes next
Maybe . . .
Then I don't see anymore

◊ ◊

We grew on a wasteland
We rain on a wasteland
We saw *Nothing* on the roads
On his winged yellow horse
he traveled the road like a king

Alas, we are happy and calm
Alas, we are sad and quiet
Happy, because we love
Sad, because love is a curse

Realizing

دریافت   *Daryāft*

In the little bubble
light was consuming itself
Suddenly night filled the window
Night overflowing with a swarm of empty voices
Night poisoned by the heat of venomous breaths
Night . . .

I listened
In the dark horrified street
it felt as if someone had squashed their heart
underfoot
like a rotten thing
In the dark horrified street
a star exploded
I listened. . . .

My pulse was swollen from the gushing of my blood
and my body. . . .
my body also
was tempted to decompose

In the crooked lines of the ceiling
I saw my own eyes
like a weighty tarantula
withering in foam, in the yellow, in suffocation

Despite all of my movements
I was silting, like stagnant water
Slowly, slowly
I was
becoming sediment in my pit

I listened
I listened to my whole life
A disgusting mouse in its hole
shamelessly singing
a stupid meaningless song
A cricket's relentless and incomprehensible chirp
turned across the fleeting moment
and drifted across the face of oblivion

Ah, I was full of lust—lust for death
Delirious, a shooting pain in my breasts
Ah
I remembered
the first day of puberty
when my whole body
opened in innocent amazement
to merge with that vague, that mute, that unknown

◊ ◊

In the little bubble
the light
yawned itself in a trembling line

Love Poem

عاشقانه   *Āsheghāneh*

O you who color my night with dreams of you
my breast fills with your scent
You who block my view
have given me more joy than sorrow
Like rain that washes the earth's body
you have cleaned the filth off my existence
O you who cause the throbbing in my burning body
and the fire in my eyes
you who are more abundant than wheat fields
more laden with fruit than golden branches
you who are, amid the dark swarm of doubts
the doorway to suns
with you I no longer fear pain
Any pain is just the pain of happiness

This sad heart of mine and this burden of light?
This tumult of living in the depths of the grave?

O you whose eyes are my meadows
your eyes have branded mine
Had you been in my heart before now
I would never have mistaken others for you
It is a dark pain, the pain of wanting
a dark pain to try and abase oneself in vain
to place one's head on dark-hearted chests
one's heart contaminated with the filth of hatreds
to feel a snakebite in every caress
to find poison in the lovers' smile
to place gold in the swindlers' hand
to become lost in the vast bazaars

Ah, you who are one with my soul
who resurrected me from my grave
who like a star with two gilded wings
came from the out-of-reach sky
and extinguished my loneliness
my body exudes the scent of your embrace
The water of you filled the dry stream of my heart
The flood of you filled the riverbeds of my veins
In a world so cold and dark
your steps lead my steps

O you, hidden under my skin
like blood boiling through my veins
whose caresses have burned my hair
and burned my cheeks with the scorch of desire
Ah, you, a stranger to my clothes
acquainted with the green meadows of my body
who are a bright never-ending daybreak
the sun of the southern lands
Ah, you more glowing than the dawn
fresher, wetter than spring
This is no longer love, it is madness
It is a chandelier in the silence and darkness
When love woke in my breast
I gave up my whole being to desire
This is no longer me, I am not
I regret the years I lived with who I was
O my lips, where your lips kiss
my eyes wait anxiously for your kiss
O you who send spasms of pleasure through my body
I wear the imprint of your body as a shirt
Ah, I want to fall entirely to pieces
For one moment I want my joy to be mixed with grief
Ah, I want to get up
and like a cloud shed torrents of tears

This sad heart and this incense smoke?
In the bedchamber, the strummings of harp and rud?
This empty space and these flights?
This silent night and these songs?

◊ ◊

O you whose gaze is for me a magic lullaby
the cradle for a sleepless infant
you whose breath blows gently over me half-asleep beside you
you have washed away my fretful tremors
you are embedded in the smile of my tomorrows
you have penetrated into the depths of my worlds

O you who have blended me with the ardor of poetry
who have poured all this fire into my poetry
because you ignited in me the fever of love
of course you have set my verse on fire

Border Walls

دیوارهای مرز   *Dīvār-hā-ye Marz*

Now, again, in the silent night
barrier walls, border walls
grow tall like plants
guardians of the fields of my love

Now, again, the filthy hubbub of the city
like an agitated school of fish
decamps from the darkness of my shore
Now, again, the windows find themselves
pleasured by the touch of diffused scents
Now all the trees asleep in the garden slip out of their bark
and through thousands of pores the soil
inhales the dizzy particles of the moon

◊ ◊

Now
come closer
and listen
to the disturbed beats of love
like the *tom-tom* of an African drum
that spreads chants through the tribe of my limbs

I sense
I know
the moment of prayer, which moment it is
Now all the stars
are making love with each other

Protected by the night I drift
from the end of all that is breeze
Protected by the night, with my heavy hair

I cascade madly
into your hands and I make a gift to you
of equatorial flowers from this young green tropical land

Come with me
Come with me to that star
to that star that for thousands of millennia
lies far from the frozen soil and empty scales of the Earth
And no one there
is afraid of light

On islands floating on the surface of the water, I breathe
I
I am looking for a piece of the vast sky
uncrowded by base thoughts

Come back to me
Come back to me
to the beginning of the body
to the fragrant center of a sperm
to the moment that I was created from you
Come back to me
I have remained incomplete because of you

Now the pigeons
take wing
above the peaks of my breasts
Now inside the cocoon of my lips
butterfly kisses contemplate flight
Now
the mehrāb of my flesh
is ready for love's worship

Come back to me
I have no words
because I love you
because "I love you" is a saying

that comes from the world of futilities
and worn-out things and repeated things
Come back to me
I have no words

Protected by the night
let me become pregnant by the moon
Let me be filled
by small drops of rain
by not-yet-developed hearts
by the form of unborn babies
Let me be filled
Maybe my love
will be the cradle for another Jesus

Friday

جمعه *Jom'eh*

Silent Friday
Deserted Friday
Friday like old miserable alleyways
Friday of lazy sick thoughts
Friday of long insidious yawns
Friday without anticipation
Friday of submission

Empty house
Depressed house
House of doors barred against the rush of youth
House of darkness, of only the idea of sun
House of loneliness and divination and doubt
House of curtains, books, cupboards, pictures

◊ ◊

Ah, how quietly and full of pride my life passed by
like an exiled stream
in the heart of these silent and deserted Fridays
in the heart of these empty and depressed houses
Ah, how quiet and full of pride it passed by. . . .

Wind-Up Doll

عروسک کوکی   *Arūsak-e Kūkī*

Longer than this, ah, yes
one can remain silent longer than this

◊ ◊

With a gaze fixed like the gaze of the dead
one can stare for long hours
into the smoke of a cigarette
at the shape of a cup
at the colorless flower in the carpet
at the faint line of writing on the wall

With withered fingers
one can draw aside the curtain and look
In the alleyway a heavy rain pours down
A child with his colorful balloons
is standing in a doorway
A worn-out cart makes a racket
as it hurries out of the empty square

One can remain in place
by the side of the curtain, but blind, deaf

With a voice utterly false, utterly foreign
one can cry out
"I love"
In the overpowering arms of a man
one can be a beautiful and healthy female
with a body like a leather tablecloth
with two big firm breasts
In the bed of a drunk, a crazy man, a tramp
one can contaminate the chastity of a love

One can belittle with cleverness
every wondrous riddle
Alone, one can do a crossword puzzle
Alone, one can amuse oneself with the discovery of a useless answer
a useless answer, yes, in five or six letters

One can kneel down for a lifetime
with head bowed, at the foot of a cold grille in a shrine
One can see God in an anonymous tomb
One can find faith with a worthless coin
One can rot in the chambers of a mosque
like an old prayer-reader
Like zero in subtraction, addition, and multiplication
one can always get the same result
One can imagine your eye in its implacable cocoon
as a colorless button on a worn-out shoe
One can, like water in its hole, dry up

With shame one can hide the beauty of a moment
like a funny black-and-white snapshot
at the bottom of a trunk
In the empty frame of what remains of the day
one can hang the image of a man condemned, defeated, or crucified
One can conceal the crack in the wall with masks
One can mingle with images emptier than these

One can be just like mechanical dolls
and see the world with two glass eyes
In a cloth-lined box
with a body filled with straw
one can sleep for years in folds of lace and sequins
With every squeeze of a lecherous hand
one can spontaneously cry out
"Ah, I'm very lucky!"

My Lover

My lover
with that shameless naked body
stood like death
on his powerful legs

In his solid figure
restless slanted lines
follow his rebellious limbs
My lover
seems to have come from forgotten generations

In the depth of his eyes
you would say a Tatar
always lies in wait to ambush a horseman
In the fresh gleam of his teeth
you would say a Berber
is drawn to the warm blood of his prey

My lover
like nature
has a clear and irresistible purpose
In the breaking of me he affirms
the true law of power
He is savagely free
like a pure instinct deep in an uninhabited island

He cleans the dust of the street
from his shoes
with shreds of Majnūn's tent

Like a god in a Nepalese temple
my lover

seems to have been a stranger
since the beginning of existence
He
is a man of past ages
a reminder of original beauty

Around him, like the scent of a baby,
he always arouses
memories of innocence
He is like a happy song of the common people
rough and raw
He loves sincerely
the particles of life
the particles of the soil
the sorrows of human beings
the pure sorrows

He loves sincerely
a village alleyway
a tree
a cup of ice cream
a clothesline

My lover
is a simple human being
a simple human being
in this inauspicious fantasy-land
whom I have hidden
like the last artifact of a wondrous religion
in the thicket of my breasts

In the Cold Streets of Night

در خیابانهای سرد شب   *Dar Khīābān-hā-ye Sard-e Shab*

I have no regrets
I am thinking of this surrender, this painful surrender
I kissed the cross of my fate
on the hills of my execution

◊ ◊

In the cold streets of night
couples always hesitate
to part from one another
In the cold streets of night
there is no sound but "Good-bye, Goodbye!"

I have no regrets
It's as if my heart flows on the far side of time
Life will repeat my heart
and the dandelion seed that floats on the lakes of the wind
will repeat me

Ah, do you see
how my skin stretches apart?
How the milk grows dense in the blue veins of my cold breasts?
How the blood
begins to form sinew in my patient womb?

I am you, you
and the one who loves
and the one who within herself
suddenly discovers a vague bonding
to a thousand things loaded with unknown strangeness
and I am all the fierce lust of the earth

that pulls all waters into itself
to make all fields fertile

Listen
to my distant voice
in the heavy mist of dawn recitations
and see me in the silence of the mirrors
how once again, with what is left of my hands
I numb the dark depth of all dreams
and I tattoo my heart, like a bloody stain
onto the innocent joys of existence

I have no regrets
Speak of me, O my lover, with the other me you will find
in the cold streets of night
with the same amorous eyes
and remember me in her sad kiss
on the sweet lines beneath your eyes

In a Never-Ending Twilight

در غروبی ابدی   *Dar Ghorūbī Abadī*

—Day or night?
—No, O friend, it is a never-ending twilight
with two pigeons passing by on the wind
like two white coffins
and voices from far away, from that alien field
vagrant and wavering, like the wind

◊ ◊

—Something must be said
Something must be said
I crave to be one with darkness
Something must be said

What a deep amnesia
An apple falls from the branch
Yellow grains of flax seeds break
in the beaks of my lovesick canaries
The fava's flower yields its blue tendrils to the intoxicating breeze
so as to escape
the vague anxiety of change
And here, in me, in my head?

Ah . . .
There is nothing in my head except the whirling of tiny thick red
    particles
and my gaze
is like a lie
downcast and ashamed

—I am thinking of a moon
—I, of a word in a poem

—I am thinking of a spring
—I, of an illusion in the soil
—I, of the rich scent of a wheat field
—I, of a fairytale about bread
—I, of the innocence of games
and of that long narrow alleyway
filled with the perfume of the acacia trees
—I, of the bitter awakening after a game
and of the bewilderment after the alleyway
and of the endless emptiness after the perfume of the acacias

◊ ◊

—Heroics?
—Ah
The horses are old
—Love?
—It is alone and from a low window looks out
at deserts missing Majnūn
at pathways that vaguely recall
a delicate ankle's languid walk, its anklets

—Desires?
—They give up
at the merciless coordination of thousands of doors
—Shut?
—Yes, always shut, shut
—You will get tired

—I am thinking of a house
with the breathing of its ivy, indolent,
with its lights, like the pupil of an eye
with its pensive nights, lazy, at ease
and of a newborn with boundless smiles
like concentric circles on the water
its body plump with blood, like a cluster of grapes
—I am thinking of its collapse

and the looting by black gusts
and of a suspicious light
that at night searches into the window
and of a small grave, small as a newborn

—Work . . . work?
—Yes, but in that big desk
lives a secret enemy
who gnaws at you very slowly
as it does the wood and the notebook
and thousands of other useless things
and in the end, you will sink in a cup of tea
like a boat in a whirlpool
and on the farthest horizon see nothing
but thick cigarette smoke
and incomprehensible lines

—A star?
—Yes, hundreds, hundreds, but
all on the far side of the walled-in nights
—A bird?
—Yes, hundreds, hundreds, but
all in distant memories
flapping their wings with useless pride
—I am thinking of a cry in the alleyway
—I, of a harmless mouse in the wall
that once in a while scrabbles by

◊ ◊

Something must be said
Something must be said
in the dawn, in the trembling moment that space
like the sensation of puberty
mixes suddenly with something vague
I want
to surrender to a rebellion

I want
to rain from that big cloud
I want
to say No No No No

—Let's go
—Something must be said
— The cup, or the bed, or loneliness, or sleep?
—Let's go. . . .

Earthly Verses

آیه های زمینی   *Āye-hā-ye Zamīnī*

Then
the sun went cold
and bounty left the lands

And the green of the fields dried up
and the fish of the seas dried up
and after that the soil rejected its dead
In all the pallid windows
night, like an uncertain image
kept crowding and rebelling
and in the darkness
the roads stopped going anywhere

No one thought about love anymore
No one thought about victory anymore
and no one
thought about anything anymore

In the caverns of loneliness
futility was born
Blood smelled of bhang and opium
Pregnant women
gave birth to headless infants
and cradles, ashamed
took shelter in graves

What bitter and black days
Bread had overcome the wondrous power of aspirations
The prophets, hungry and wrecked
fled from their trysts with God
and to the bewilderment of the fields
the lost lambs no longer heard

the shepherds' call of "Hey, Hey!"
In the eyes of the mirrors it seemed
that movements and colors and images
were reflected upside down
and above the heads of lowlife clowns
and the shameless faces of whores
a bright holy halo burned
like a flaming parasol

With those vapors of bitter poison
alcohol swamps sucked down
into their depths
the paralyzed crowd of intellectuals
and in the old closet
the sly mice gnawed
the gilded pages of the books

The sun had died
The sun had died, and *tomorrow*
in the minds of children
had a vague lost meaning
They portrayed the strangeness of this ancient word
in their exercise books
with a large black dot

People
the crowd of fallen people
discouraged and emaciated and dazed
burdened with their inauspicious corpses
went from exile to exile
and the painful desire for crime
swelled in their hands

Sometimes a spark, a meager spark
from within
suddenly shattered
this silent and lifeless gathering

They fell upon one another
Men cut open each other's throats
with knives
and had sex in a bed of blood
with prepubescent girls

They drowned in their own terror
and the fear of sin had paralyzed
their blind dull souls

Always, in the execution ceremony
when the noose's pressure squeezed
the spasming eyes of the condemned
out from his skull
they would be deeply moved
and their old and tired nerves
twitched with lust

But always at the edges of the squares
you saw these petty criminals
who stand
and stare
at the stubborn flowing of the fountains

◊ ◊

And perhaps, still
behind crushed eyes, in the frozen depths
one half-alive confused thing
had remained in place
which in its powerless struggle wanted to believe
in the purity of the waters' song

Perhaps, but what endless emptiness
The sun had died
and no one knew
that the name of that sad pigeon

who had flown from every heart
was *Faith*

◊ ◊

Ah, O imprisoned voice
won't the splendor of your despair
dig a tunnel out of this hateful night
in any direction
toward the light?
Ah, O imprisoned voice
O last voice of voices. . . .

Gift

هديه   *Hedyeh*

I speak from the limit of night
I speak from the limit of darkness
and of the limit of night

If you come to my house, O kind one, bring me a lamp
and a tiny opening through which
I might look at the crowd in the happy street

Green Illusion

وهم سبز   *Vahm-e Sabz*

All day I cried in the mirror
Spring had entrusted my window
to the green illusion of the trees
My body no longer fit the cocoon of my loneliness
and the stink of my paper crown
had contaminated the air of that sunless realm

◊ ◊

I couldn't, I couldn't anymore
The sounds of the alleyway, the sound of birds
the sound of tennis balls bouncing away
and the fleeting uproar of children
and the dance of balloons
rising to the end of their string stems
like soap bubbles
and the wind, the wind that panted as if it was far down
in the deepest dark moments of sex—
all these assaulted the silent fortress-wall of my confidence
and, through old fissures, called out to my heart by name

All day my gaze
was fixed on the eyes of my life
on those two anxious fearful eyes
that fled from my fixed stare
and like liars
sought refuge in the safe sanctuary of their lids

◊ ◊

Which summit? Which heights?
Don't all these winding roads

converge and end
in that cold sucking mouth?
O words that deceive simple people
O denial of the body's desires, what did you give me?
If I had placed a rose in my hair
wouldn't it have been more alluring
than this fraud, this paper crown
that stinks on the top of my head?

◊ ◊

How the spirit of the wild captured me
and the magic of the moon made me stray from the faith of the flock!
How my unfilled heart swelled
and no other half made it whole!
How I stood and saw
the earth under my two feet give way
and how the heat of my lover's body
never found its way to my body, waiting in vain!

Which summit? Which heights?
Shelter me O confused lamps
O bright doubting houses
where, in the arms of fragrant smoke
clean laundry swings on sunny rooftops

Shelter me O simple complete women
whose delicate fingertips trace, through the skin
the thrilling movement of the fetus
and in whose blouse-folds the air
is always mixed with the scent of fresh milk

Which summit? Which heights?
Shelter me O fire-filled hearths—O lucky horseshoes—
and O song of blackened copper kitchen-pots
and O depressing hum of the sewing machine
and O ongoing battle between carpets and brooms

Shelter me O all greedy loves
whose painful desire for perpetuity adorns the bed of your conquests
with magic water
and drops of fresh blood

◊ ◊

All day, all day
cast off, cast off, like a corpse on the water
I was heading toward the most terrifying rocks
toward the deepest caverns of the sea
and the most carnivorous fish
and my delicate vertebrae
sensing death, flinched with pain

I couldn't, I couldn't any longer
The sound of my footsteps arose from the road's refusal
and my despair expanded beyond the patience of my soul
and that spring, that green illusion
that passed by the shutters, said to my heart:
"Look
you never moved forward
you sank."

Pair

جفت   *Joft*

Evening comes
and after evening, darkness
and after darkness
eyes
hands
and breaths   breaths   breaths . . .
and the sound of water
that pours down   drip   drip   drip   from the tap

◊ ◊

Then two red dots
from two lit cigarettes
the tick-tock of the clock
and two hearts
and two solitudes

The Victory of the Garden

فتح باغ   *Fat-he Bāgh*

That crow that flew
above our heads
and into the turbulent thoughts of a wandering cloud
whose call, like a short spear, traveled the breadth of the horizon
will carry our news to the city

◊ ◊

Everyone knows
Everyone knows
that from that cold sullen window
you and I have seen the garden
and have picked the apple
from that playful branch beyond our reach

Everyone is afraid
Everyone is afraid, but you and I
became one with the lamp and the water and the mirror
and were not afraid

This is not about the flimsy linking of two names
having sex in the pages of an old ledger
This is about my lucky hair
the burnt poppies of your kiss
the intimacy of our bodies in the slipperiness
and iridescence of our nakedness
like fish scales in water
This is about the silvery life of the song
that the little fountain sings at dawn

One night we asked the wild hares
in that flowing green forest

and the pearl-filled shells
in that turbulent cold-blooded sea
and the young eagles
on that solitary victorious mountain
what should be done

Everyone knows
Everyone knows
we have found the way to the cold and silent dream of the sīmorghs
we have found the truth in the garden
in the shy glance of a nameless flower
and eternity in an infinite moment
when two suns gazed at one another

This is not about fearful whispering in the darkness
This is about day and open windows
and fresh breeze
and a stove in which useless things are burning
and an earth that bears fruit from a different planting
and birth and evolving and pride
This is about our loving hands
that from the message of scent and light and breeze
have built a bridge that spans the nights

Come to the meadow
Come to the great meadow
and call to me, from behind the breath of the silk tree
as the deer calls to his mate

The curtains overflow with hidden spite
and the innocent pigeons
from the heights of their white tower
look down at the earth

Rose

گل سرخ *Gol-e Sorkh*

Red rose
Red rose
Red rose

He took me to the rose garden
and in darkness placed a red rose in my agitated hair
and in the end
on the petal of a red rose he slept with me

O paralyzed pigeons
O inexperienced menopausal trees, O blind windows
a red rose is growing
red rose
red
like a flag in
an uprising

Ah, I am pregnant, pregnant, pregnant

The Bird Was Just a Bird

پرنده فقط یک پرنده بود   *Parandeh Faghat Yek Parandeh Būd*

The bird said: "What a scent, what a sun, ah
spring has come
and I will go search for my mate."

From the balcony's railing the bird
flew, flew away like a message

The bird was small
The bird didn't think
The bird didn't read the newspaper
The bird had no debt
The bird didn't know people

The bird flew on the air
and above the traffic lights
in the heights of unawareness
and experienced madly
the blue moments

The bird, ah, was just a bird

O Jeweled Land

ای مرز پر گوهر   *Ey Marz-e Por Gohar*

Victory!
I registered myself
I adorned myself with a name, on an ID card
my existence distinguished with a number
So hail to #678, issued at Precinct 5, Resident of Tehran!
Now I don't have to worry anymore
The kind bosom of the Motherland
the pacifier of the past full of the glory of history
the lullaby of civilization and culture
the squeaky-toy of the law . . .
Ah,
now I don't have to worry anymore

Overwhelmed with joy
I went to the window and eagerly inhaled
six hundred and seventy-eight times
deep deep into my lungs
air thick with manure and the scent of garbage and piss
and at the bottom of six hundred and seventy-eight invoices
and on the face of six hundred and seventy-eight job application forms
I wrote *Forough Farrokhzad*

Now that, after years and years, the reality of your existence has been
    acknowledged
it's a gift to live
in the land of poetry and the rose and the nightingale
a place where
with my first official look through the curtain, I see six-hundred and
    seventy-eight poets
impostors, in the guise of strange beggars
searching through garbage for meter and rhyme

a place where six hundred and seventy-eight mysterious nightingales who
suddenly, for amusement, have taken the form of six hundred and
    seventy-eight old black crows
at the sound of my first official step
fly lazily from dark swamps
toward the edge of day
a place where my first official breath is mixed
with the scent of six hundred and seventy-eight red roses
fresh from the great PLASCO factory

Yes, it's a gift to live
in the birthplace of Sheikh Abū Clown, the junkie kamāncheh-player
and Sheikh "O Love, O Love," a tombak in the tanbūr family
to live in in the city of fat superstars—legs, hips, boobs on the cover of *Art*
in the cradle of those who compile the philosophy of "Phooey, who cares?"
the cradle of the IQ Olympics—yeah!
a place where, from every regular media outlet, video or audio
comes the blare of the genius of this year's new geniuses
And as for the intelligentsia of the nation
they sit in their adult literacy class
each holding close to his chest six hundred and seventy-eight electric
    kabob cookers
and displaying on his wrist six hundred and seventy-eight Navzer
    watches and they know
that weakness arises from an empty pocket, not from ignorance

Victory! Yes, victory!
Now to celebrate this victory
in front of the mirror I proudly light six hundred and seventy-eight
    candles bought on credit
and I jump up on the window seat in order that I may, with your kind
    permission, say a few words
on the subject of the legal advantages of such a life
and so that with with a pickaxe I may, to the sound of passionate applause
break ground for the very tall building of my life
with a single blow to the crown of my head

I am alive, yes, as the Zāyandeh River was once alive
and from all that is the monopoly of the living I will take my share

Starting tomorrow I will be able to go forth strolling
through city streets brimful of the nation's bounty
among the slender shadows of the telephone poles
and proudly I will write six hundred and seventy-eight times on the
    walls of the public bathrooms
I WRITE THIS TO MAKE ASSES LAUGH

Starting tomorrow like a zealous patriot
I will be able to cherish
in heart and mind
a share in the Grand Ideal Lottery
held every Wednesday afternoon
followed eagerly and anxiously by all
a share of those 1,000-riyal notes that nurture a thousand desires
that can be used for the purchase of refrigerators and furniture and
    curtains
or exchanged for six hundred seventy-eight real votes
that can be donated one night to six hundred and seventy-eight
    patriotic men

Starting tomorrow
in the back room of Khachik the Armenian's shop
after having a few snorts of first-rate product
and a goblet of doctored Pepsi Cola
and after scattering a few "Yā-Haqq!"s and "Yā-Hū!"s and "Bowwow!"s
    and "Hoo-Hoo!"s
I will be able to join the gathering of learned thinkers and intellectual
    chickenshits
and the followers of the school of thug dancing
and sometime around the 1,678th year of Shams-e Tabrīzī
the first draft of my big novel
will be printed by a bankrupt press on both sides of six hundred and
    seventy-eight packets
of OSHNU genuine special cigarettes

Starting tomorrow with complete confidence,
I will be able to invite myself to sit in a velvet-covered throne through
    six hundred and seventy-eight sessions
of the Majles of the Gathering for Securing the Future
or the Majles of Thanks and Praise
because I have read every issue of *Art & Science* and *Homage & Flattery*
and I understand the skill of "Writing Correctly"

I have stepped into the space of existence where the creative masses live
and although no bread can be found there
it offers a field of wide-open vision
its actual geography defined
to the north by the fresh green of Bullet Square
to the south by Execution Square
and by Artillery Square in the center of town

And from dawn until sunset, in the shelter of a shining and safe sky
six hundred and seventy-eight plaster swans
along with six hundred and seventy-eight angels
—angels made of mixed dirt and mud, by the way—
are busy proceeding with plans for stillness and silence

◊ ◊

Victory! Yes, victory!
So hail to #678, issued by Precinct 5, Resident of Tehran
who thanks to perseverance and willpower
has reached such an elevated station that she now stands quietly
in the window frame
six hundred and seventy-eight meters above the ground

and boasts of this:
that she can from this very small opening—not by way of the stairs—
throw herself head-over-heels madly into the lap of the kind
    Motherland

and her last will and testament requests
that in exchange for six hundred and seventy-eight coins Master
   Teacher Abraham Sabhā
write an elegy in some bullshit rhyme praising her life

I Will Greet the Sun Again

به آفتاب سلامی دوباره خواهم داد

Beh Āftāb Salāmī Dobāreh Khāham Dād

I will greet the sun again
I will greet
the stream that flowed in me
the clouds that were my long thoughts
the painful growth of the aspens in the garden
who passed with me through the dry seasons
I will greet the flock of crows
who brought me the scent of the fields at night
as a gift
I will greet my mother who lived in the mirror
and was the reflection of my old age
and greet the earth again
whose throbbing interior, with my chronic lust
I have stuffed with green seeds

I will come, I will come, I will come
with my glossy hair: rich with the scents of turned-up soil
with my eyes: experiences of thick darkness
with bushes I have picked from the grove on the other side of the wall
I will come, I will come, I will come
and the threshold will be filled with love
and on the threshold
I will greet those who love again
and the girl still standing there
on the love-filled threshold

Another Birth

تولدی دیگر   *Tavallodi Dīgar*

My whole being is a dark verse
that by repeating you in itself
will carry you to the dawn of eternal blossoming and growth
In this verse I sighed you
ah, in this verse
I grafted you to tree and water and fire

◊ ◊

Maybe life
is a long street in which every day a woman with a basket passes by
Maybe life
is a rope with which a man hangs himself from a branch
Maybe life is a young child coming home from school

Maybe life is lighting a cigarette in the languid pause between making
    love and making love again
or the distracted gait of a passer-by
who lifts his hat from his head
and with a meaningless smile says to another passer-by, "Good morning"

Maybe life is that enclosed moment
in which my gaze annihilates itself in the pupils of your eyes
and in this there is a feeling that I will mix
with the moon's understanding and the acceptance of darkness

In a room the size of a loneliness
my heart
the size of a love
looks for simple excuses for happiness
to the beautiful wilting of the flowers in the vase
to the sapling you planted in the garden of our house

and to the song of the canaries
who sing the size of a window

Ah . . .
This is my lot
This is my lot
My lot
is a sky that the pulling of a curtain takes away from me
My lot is to descend an abandoned stairway
and join something rotting and in exile
My lot is a walk stained with grief in the garden of memories
and to die grieving for the voice that says to me
"I love
your hands"

I bury my hands in the garden
I will grow, I know, I know, I know
and swallows will lay their eggs
in the hollow of my ink-stained fingers

I hang twin red cherries
over my ears as earrings
and stick dahlia petals on my fingernails
There is an alleyway where
the boys who were in love with me
with the same tousled hair and skinny necks and spindly legs
are still thinking of the innocent smiles of a girl who was carried away
one night
by the wind

There is an alleyway that my heart
has stolen from the neighborhoods of my youth

The journey of a form along the line of time
a form impregnating the barren line of time
a form conscious of an image
that returns from a feast in a mirror

And thus it is
that someone dies
and someone remains

◊ ◊

No fisherman will find a pearl in the humble stream that pours into a pit

I
know a sad little fairy
who lives in an ocean
and plays her heart out softly, softly
on a pennywhistle
a sad little fairy
who dies with a kiss at night
and is born with a kiss at dawn

Let Us Believe in the Beginning of the Cold Season

ایمان بیاوریم به آغاز فصل سرد

Īmān Bīāvarīm Beh Āghāz-e Fasl-e Sard

And here I am
a woman alone
at the threshold of a cold season
about to understand the contaminated existence of the earth
and the sky's simple and sad despair
and the powerlessness of these concrete hands

Time passed
Time passed and the cuckoo clock struck four
struck four
Today is the winter solstice
I know the seasons' secret
and understand each moment
The savior lies in his tomb
and the soil, the inviting soil
suggests peace

Time passed and the clock struck four

In the street the wind is blowing
In the street the wind is blowing
and I am thinking about the flowers mating
about buds on thin anemic legs
and this exhausted, tubercular time
and a man
is passing by the soaked trees
the man whose threads of blue veins, like dead snakes
have crawled up the two sides of his throat
and repeat into his panic those bloody syllables:

"Hello!"
"Hello!"
and I am thinking about the flowers mating

At the threshold of a cold season
among the mirrors gathered in mourning
and the huddled experiences, grieving and pale
and in this sunset pregnant by the knowledge of silence
how can one command that person passing by
patient
heavy
confused
to stop?
How can one tell that man he is not alive, that he has never lived

In the street the wind is blowing
and the isolated crows of solitude
circle in the old gardens of apathy
and the ladder
how stubby it is

They took all the heart's gullibility
with them to the castle of fairytales
and now after this
how would someone get up to dance
and cast her childhood curls
into the rushing waters
and crush underfoot the apple
that she has finally picked and smelled?

O my love, my most unique love
such clouds of darkness lie in wait for the sun's feast day

It's as if on an imagined flight path one day that bird appeared
as if those new leaves panting under the breeze's lust
were green lines of imagination

as if
that violet flame burning in the pure mind of the windows
was nothing but an innocent fantasy about the lamp

In the street the wind is blowing
This is the beginning of ruin
On that day when your hands were ruined the wind was blowing too
Dear stars
dear cardboard stars
when lies start to blow around in heaven
how can one take refuge in the suras of shamed prophets?
Like the thousands of thousands of years-old dead we will find one
    another and then
it will be the sun who will pass judgment on the decay of our corpses

I'm cold
I'm cold and I will never be warm
O my love, my most unique love, "How old was that wine?"
See how heavy time is
right here
and how the fish chew my flesh
Why do you always hold me down at the bottom of the sea?

I'm cold and I hate mother-of-pearl earrings
I'm cold and I know
that of all the crimson fantasies of one wild poppy
nothing will remain
but a few drops of blood

I shall give up writing lines
as I shall give up counting numbers
and in the midst of defined geometrical forms
I shall take refuge in the vast expanse of the senses
I am naked, naked, naked
Like the silences between lovers' words I am naked
and my wounds are all from love
from love, love, love

I have guided this wandering island safely
past the turbulence of the ocean
and the volcano's eruption
and being multiple was the secret of that fused existence
and from its tiniest particles the sun was born

Hello, O innocent night!

Hello, O night, who changes the eyes of desert wolves
into bony sockets of faith and trust
On the banks of your streams the souls of willows
smell the kind souls of axes
I come from the world of indifferent thoughts and words and voices
and this world resembles a nest of snakes
and this world is filled with the sound of the footsteps of people
who as they kiss you
mentally braid the rope for your hanging

Hello, O innocent night!

Between the window and seeing
there is always a gap
Why didn't I look?
Like that time when a man was passing by the soaked trees . . .

Why didn't I look?
It seemed my mother had wept that night
that night I met pain and the seed took form
the night I became the bride of the acacia clusters
the night Esfahān was full of the tinkling of glazed blue tiles
and that one who was my other half had returned within my seed
and in the mirror I saw him
clean and bright as a mirror
and suddenly he called me
and I became the bride of the acacia clusters. . . .

It seemed my mother had wept that night
What useless light leaked from behind the small closed door
Why didn't I look?
All the moments of happiness knew
that your hands would be ruined
and I didn't look
until the little door on the clock
opened and that sad canary sang four times
sang four times
and I met that little woman whose eyes
like empty sīmorgh nests
rolled up as her pumping thighs
carried the virginity of my glorious dream
with her to the bed of night

Will I ever again
comb my hair in the wind?
Will I ever again plant violets in the gardens?
And place geraniums
in the sky beyond the window?
Will I ever again dance across wine glasses?
Will the doorbell ever again lead me to expect a voice?

I said to my mother: "It's over."
I said: "It happens before you know it.
We must send our condolences to the newspaper."

Hollow one
Hollow complacent one
Look at how his teeth
sing a song when he chews
and how his eyes
devour when they stare
and how he is passing by the soaked trees
patient
heavy
confused

At four o'clock
at the moment when his threads of blue veins, like dead snakes
have crawled up the two sides of his throat
and repeat into his panic those bloody syllables:
"Hello!"
"Hello!"
Have you
ever smelled
those four blue tulips?...

Time passed
Time passed and night fell on the naked branches of the acacias
Night slid down behind the window sucking down
with its cold tongue
the remains of the vanished day

Where do I come from?
Where do I come from?
That I reek of the smell of night?
The soil of his grave is still fresh
I mean the grave of those two young green hands. . . .

How tender you were, O my love, O my most unique love
How tender you were when you lied
How tender you were when you closed the eyelids of the mirrors
and plucked the chandeliers from their wiry stems
and in the cruel darkness led me up to the pasture of love
until that giddy mist that followed the fire of thirst
settled over the meadow of sleep

And those cardboard stars
were swirling around the infinite
Why did they use a voice to speak?
Why did they invite a sultry glance into the house of seeing?
Why did they bring a caress
to the modesty of virgin hair?
Look here

how the soul of the one who spoke with words
and whose glance was kind
and whose caress calmed the runaway
was crucified
on the crossbeams of superstition
and how the branch-marks of your fingers
like the five letters of *truth*
remain there on his cheek

What is silence, what, what, O my most unique love?
What is silence but unspoken words?
I can no longer speak but the language of sparrows
is the language that lives in the flowing sentences of nature's celebra-
tion
The language of sparrows means: spring   leaf   spring
The language of sparrows means: breeze   scent   breeze
The language of sparrows dies in the factory

Who is this, this one traveling the road of eternity
toward the moment of oneness
whose perpetual watch is wound
with mathematically logical subtractions and discord?
Who is this, this one who doesn't recognize
that the rooster's call opens the day's heart
who thinks only that it signals the first smell of breakfast?
Who is this, this one who wears love's crown
and has rotted away among the wedding dresses?

And so the sun, in the end, didn't shine
at a single moment
on both hopeless poles

You became empty of the tinkling of glazed blue tiles

And I am so accomplished that they are praying on the platform of my
    voice . . .

Lucky corpses
depressed corpses
quiet pensive corpses
social corpses, well-groomed, finely-fed
in the stations of fixed schedules
against a suspicious background of temporary lights
lusting to buy the rotten fruits of futility . . .
Ah
how many people there are, worried about an accident at intersections
and the sound of police whistles
at the moment when there must, there must, there must
be a man crushed under the wheels of this time
the man who is passing by the soaked trees . . .

Where do I come from?

I said to my mother: "It's over."
I said: "It happens before you know it.
We must send our condolences to the newspaper."

Hello, O strange loneliness
I surrender the room to you
because the dark clouds
are always prophets bringing new purifying verses
and in the martyrdom of one candle
is the illuminated secret that the last
and longest-lasting flame knows well

Let us believe
Let us believe in the beginning of the cold season
Let us believe in the ruined gardens of imagination
in the scythe hanging upside down and idle
and the incarcerated seeds
Look at how hard the snow is falling. . . .

Perhaps the truth was those two young hands, those two young hands

that were buried under the continually falling snow
and next year, when spring
makes love with the sky beyond the window
and in its body fountains of feathery green stalks bubble up
it will blossom, O my love, O my most unique love

Let us believe in the beginning of the cold season . . .

After You

بعد از تو   *Ba'd Az To*

O my seventh year, the year I turned seven
O wondrous moment of departure
After you everything that happened, happened in a mass of craziness and
   insanity

After you the window that had been such a vivid and bright connection
between the bird and us
between the wind and us
      broke
               broke
                       broke
After you that clay doll that said nothing
nothing but water, water, water
drowned in water

After you we killed the voice of the cicada
and became attached
to the sound of the school bell rising over our ABCs
and to the whistle of factories

After you our play space that had been under tables moved
from beneath the tables
to behind desks
and from behind desks
to the tops of desks
and we played at the tables and lost
We lost your colors, O my seventh year

After you we betrayed each other
After you we erased all the scrawled memories
from the plastered temple walls of the alleyway
with bullets and

blood spatter
After you we went to the squares
and screamed
"Long live..."
"Death to..."
and in the square's uproar we applauded for the little singing coins
that had cleverly come into town for a visit

After you we murdered each other
We judged for love
and while our hearts
sat uneasily in our pockets
we judged in love's name

After you we set off for the cemeteries
and Death was breathing under grandmother's chador
and Death was that enormous tree
where on this side of the beginning the living
were tying cloth wishes to its exhausted branches
and on the far side of the end the dead
were clawing at its phosphorescent roots
and Death was seated atop the holy tomb
and at each of its corners suddenly a blue tulip lamp
flared

I hear the sound of the wind
I hear the sound of the wind, O my seventh year

I got up and drank water
and suddenly I remembered
how your newly planted fields feared the swarm of locusts
How much must be paid?
How much must be paid
to grow this concrete cube?

Whatever had to be lost we lost
We set out without a lamp

and the moon, the moon, the kind feminine moon, was always there
in our childhood memory of a mud-and-thatch-plastered roof
and above those newly planted fields that feared the swarms of locusts

How much must be paid?

Window

پنجره *Panjareh*

A window for seeing
A window for hearing
A window like a well
that ends deep in the heart of the earth
and opens out into this expanse of recurring blue kindness
A window that overfills the tiny hands of loneliness
with its nightly gift, the perfume of generous stars
and from there
one could invite the sun to the geraniums in exile
One window is enough for me

I come from the land of dolls
from under the shade of paper trees
in the garden of a picture book
from the dry seasons of barren friendship and love
in the dusty alleyways of innocence
from the years the letters of the colorless alphabet grew
behind the school's tubercular desks
from the moment the children could write
the word "stone" on the blackboard
and the panicked starlings flushed from the ancient tree

I come from among the roots of carnivorous plants
and my brain is still overflowing
with the terrified voice of the butterfly
they crucified in a notebook
with a pin

When my trust hung suspended by the thin rope of justice
and all over town
they were chopping up the heart of my lamps
when they bound the childish eyes of my love

with the black blindfold of the law
and from the agitated temples of my desire
spurts of blood were scattering everywhere
when my life was nothing more
nothing more than the tick-tock of the wall clock
I realized I must, I must, I must
love madly

One window is enough for me
A window on to the moment of awareness and seeing and silence
Now the walnut sapling
has grown tall enough to tell its young leaves
the meaning of the wall
Ask the mirror
the name of your savior
Isn't the earth, trembling under your feet
lonelier than you are?
The prophets brought their prophecy of desolation
with them into our century
The ongoing detonations
and the poisoned clouds
are these the reverberations of holy verses?
O friend, O brother, O my kin
when you arrive at the moon
write the history of the mass murder of the flowers

Dreams are always
thrown down from the heights of their own naïveté
I smell a four-leaf clover
that has grown on the gravestone of worn-out meanings
Was the woman buried in her shroud of waiting and chastity
    my own youth?
Will I again climb the stairs of my own curiosity
to greet the good God strolling on the roof?

I sense time has passed
I sense that "the moment" is my share of the leaves of history

I sense that the table is an illusory gap between my hair and the hands of
    this sad stranger

Say something to me
What does one who grants you the kindness of a living body
want from you in return but an understanding of what it means to feel
    alive?

Say something to me
In the sanctuary of my window
I am one with the sun

I Pity the Garden

دلم برای باغچه میسوزد   *Delam Barā-ye Bāghcheh Mīsūzad*

No one is thinking about the flowers
No one is thinking about the fish
No one wants
to believe that the garden is dying
that the heart of the garden has swollen under the sun
that the mind of the garden is slowly, slowly
being emptied of green memories
and it's as if the garden's feelings
are a nothing rotting in isolation in the garden

Our courtyard is lonely
Our courtyard yawns
waiting for the rain from an anonymous cloud
and our pool is empty
Tiny inexperienced stars
fall to earth from the heights of the trees
and at night, from the pallid windows of the fishpond
comes the sound of coughing
Our courtyard is lonely

Father says:
"It's over for me
It's over for me
I did what I had to
and finished my job"
and in his room from dawn to sunset
he reads either the *Book of Kings*
or the *History to End All Histories*
Father says to Mother:
"To hell with every fish and fowl
When I die
what difference will it make if there is a garden

or if there is not a garden?
For me, my pension is enough."

Mother's whole life
is a prayer mat spread out
on the threshold of the horrors of Hell
Mother always searches at the bottom of everything
for traces of sin's footprint
and thinks that the blasphemy of a single plant
has contaminated the garden
Mother prays all day long
Mother is by nature a sinner
and blesses all the flowers
and blesses all the fish
and blesses herself
Mother is waiting for the arrival of the Mahdī
and His forgiveness

My brother calls the garden a cemetery
My brother laughs at the riot of weeds
and inventories the fish corpses
that under the sick skin of the water
decompose into bits of putrefaction
My brother is addicted to philosophy
My brother thinks the cure for the garden
is the destruction of the garden
He gets drunk
and, drunk, punches everything
and tries to say
that he is so afflicted and exhausted and desperate
He carries his despair with him
into the street and the bazaar
as well as his ID and calendar and handkerchief and lighter and pen
and his despair
is so small that each night
it gets lost in the crowd at the tavern

And my sister, who was the flowers' friend
who, when Mother hit her
brought her heart's simple words to their kind and silent company
and sometimes treated the family of fish
to sun and sweets . . .
Her house is on the other side of the city
She, in her artificial house
with her artificial goldfish
in the shelter of her artificial husband
and beneath the branches of her artificial apple trees
sings artificial songs
and produces real babies
Whenever she comes to see us
and the hem of her skirt is stained by the poor garden
she
bathes in eau de cologne
Whenever she comes to see us
she
is pregnant

Our courtyard is lonely
Our courtyard is lonely
All day long
from behind the door comes the sound of chopping
and explosions
Instead of flowers all of our neighbors are planting
grenades and machine guns in their gardens
All of our neighbors have covered
the tops of their tiled pools
and now the tiled pools
given no choice
are caches of hidden gunpowder
and the children of our alleyway
have filled their school backpacks with little bombs
Our courtyard is confused

I fear the time
that has lost its heart
I fear the idea of all these useless hands
and the appearance and strangeness of all these faces
I, like a school child
who loves her geometry lessons madly
am alone
and I think the garden could be taken to the hospital
I think . . .
I think . . .
I think . . .
and the heart of the garden has swollen under the sun
and the mind of the garden is slowly, slowly
being emptied of green memories

Someone Who Is Like No One

کسی که مثل هیچکس نیست   *Kasī Keh Mesl-e Hīchkas Nīst*

I dreamed that someone is coming
I dreamed of a red star
and my eyelids keep twitching
and my shoes always land as a pair
and may I go blind
if I'm lying
I dreamed of that red star
when I wasn't asleep
Someone is coming
Someone is coming
Someone different
Someone better
Someone who is not like anyone, not like Father, not like Ensī, not like
     Yahyā, not like Mother
and is as he should be
and is taller than the trees around the bricklayer's house
and his face
is even brighter than the face of the Mahdī
and he is not even afraid of Seyyed Javād's brother
who went and put on a policeman's uniform
and he is not even afraid of Seyyed Javād himself who owns all rooms in
     our house
and his name, as Mother calls him
at the beginning of her prayers and at the end of her prayers
is either The Judge of Judges
or He Who Grants Every Need
and he can read
all the hard words in a third-grade book
with his eyes closed
and not only that, he can take away a thousand from twenty million
and not come up short
and he can get whatever he needs from Seyyed Javād's store on credit

and he can do something to make the neon sign that said ALLAH
that was green green as the dawn
shine again in the sky above the Meftāhyān Mosque
Ah . . .
How good light is
How good light is
and how much I wish that
Yahyā
might have a pushcart
with a kerosene lamp
and how much I wish
I might sit in Yahyā's cart among the watermelons and the muskmelons
and ride around Mohammadyeh Square
Ah . . .
How good it is to ride around the square
How good it is to sleep on the roof
How good it is to go to Mellī Park
How good Pepsi tastes
How good it is to watch Fardīn's movies
and how much I enjoy all these good things
and how much I want to pull
Seyyed Javād's daughter's hair

Why am I so little
that I get lost in the streets
Why doesn't Father who is not so little
and who doesn't get lost in the streets
do something to hurry up the coming of the person I saw in my dream
And the people in the slaughterhouse district
where even the soil of their gardens is bloody
and even the water in their pools is bloody
and even the soles of their shoes are bloody
why don't they do something?
Why don't they do something?

How lazy the winter sun is

I have swept the stairs up to the roof
and I have even washed the window panes
Why does Father only
dream when he's sleeping?

I have swept the stairs up to the roof
and I have even washed the window panes

Someone is coming
Someone is coming
Someone is coming who in his heart is with us, who in his breath is with us,
    who in his voice is with us

Someone's arrival
can't be arrested
and handcuffed and thrown in prison
Someone who had children under Yahyā's old clothes
children who day by day
grow and get bigger
Someone from the rain, from the sound of pouring rain, from among the
    whispering petunias

Someone is coming from Tūpkhāneh's sky on the night of the fireworks
and spreads out the picnic cloth
and distributes the bread
and distributes the Pepsis
and distributes Mellī Park
and distributes the syrup for whooping cough
and distributes the registration days for school
and distributes the hospital priority numbers
and distributes the rubber boots
and distributes tickets to Fardīn's movies
He distributes the dresses of Seyyed Javād's daughter
and distributes everything that is left over
and also gives us our share
I dreamed . . .

Only the Sound Remains

تنها صداست که میماند   *Tanhā Sedāst Ke Mīmānad*

Why should I stop, why?
The birds have left to look for a place by water
The horizon is vertical
The horizon is vertical and motion is like a fountain
and within the limits of vision
the bright planets spin
Earth at its apogee begins to repeat itself
and pockets in the air
become escape tunnels of connection
and the day is an expanse
that won't fit into the narrow mind of the newspaper-worm

Why should I stop?
The road passes along the capillaries of life
The quality of the space
in the ship of the moon's womb
will kill the rotten cells
and after sunrise, in the chemical-laden air
only the sound remains
the sound that will be absorbed by the tiny particles of time
Why should I stop?

What can a swamp be
What can a swamp be but a spawning-ground for insects of corruption
Swollen corpses write the morgue's thoughts
The coward
has hidden the loss of his manhood in the dark
and the beetle . . . ah!
when the beetle speaks
why should I stop?
Cooperation among letters of lead type is futile
Cooperation among letters of lead type

will never rescue petty thoughts
I am descended from the trees
Breathing stale air exhausts me
A dead bird advised me to remember flight

The most perfect of powers is to connect, to connect
with the luminous sun
and to become one with the light's intelligence
It is the nature of windmills
to decay
Why should I stop?
I hold sheaves of unripe wheat
to my breasts
and give them milk

The sound, the sound, only the sound
the sound of the water's transparent wish to flow
the sound of starlight pouring over the skin of the feminine earth
the sound of the conjunction of the sperm of truth
and the growth of the shared mind of love
the sound, the sound, the sound, it's only the sound that remains

In the land of short people
the standards of measurement
have always traveled in the orbit of zero
Why should I stop?
I obey the four elements
and drafting the rules of my heart
is not the business of the local council of the blind

What's it to me, the long savage howl
of the animal's genitals
What's it to me, the movement of the lowly worm in the meaty void
The bloody lineage of the flowers has bound me to life
Do you know the bloody lineage of the flowers?

The Bird Is Mortal

پرنده مردنی است   *Parandeh Mordanīst*

I am depressed
I am depressed

I go out on the verandah and run my fingers
across the taut skin of the night
The lamps of connection have gone dark
The lamps of connection have gone dark

No one will introduce me
to the sun
No one will take me to the sparrows' party
Remember its flight
because the bird is mortal

Notes

4   *If I choose silence*: The noun "silence" in Persian plays on the verb that means "to extinguish (a candle)."

16   *Kāmī*. This is the diminutive and intimate nickname for her son, Kāmyār.

17   *Zohreh*: Hārūt and Mārūt were among the angels that protested to God that people on earth were being permitted to sin without adequate punishment. God decided to let them try and resist such temptations and sent them to Babylon (Surah 2:101). They became entranced with a beautiful woman named Zohreh, who plied them with alcohol, seduced them, and tricked them into revealing the greatest name of God, by means of which she turned herself into the star, Venus.

22   *korsī*: On winter nights a brazier of coals covered with ash was set beneath a table in the central room; the table was covered with a blanket or quilt, providing warmth for the room and the people sleeping in it.

    checkmarks from my old exercise books: Elementary school teachers crossed out students' work with a long, diagonal line on pages that had been reviewed. Often students tried to erase the markings so as to present their copying or handwriting exercises as new work.

23   *the simple language of dandelions*: The fluffy seeds of dandelions were thought to carry, through the air, messages of love to one's beloved.

28   *the pale silent dots / on the mixed-up letters of madness*: The Persian alphabet consists of a certain number of shapes. Individual letters are distinguished by the number and placement of dots above or below the shape.

35   *Love Poem*: This translation is dedicated to Farrokh Anvar.

39   *mehrāb*: Niche in the wall of a mosque indicating the direction toward Mecca, the direction of prayer.

41   *Friday*: The Islamic equivalent of the Sabbath, the holy day of the week.

43   *One can see God in an anonymous tomb*: This stanza draws on images of worship at various shrines found in Iran. The tomb of the holy person is surrounded and protected by an enclosure, usually a grille of silver, to which pilgrims and worshippers can tie wishes and through which they can throw coins. A pilgrim who is unable to read will often pay a person at or around the shrine to recite the appropriate prayers.

44   *Majnūn*: In classical poet Nezāmī's romantic epic, *Leylī and Majnūn* (12th century.), the poet Qeys, forbidden by her father to marry Leylī, goes mad (*majnūn*) and spends the rest of his life wandering and camping in the desert singing poems to her. See also page 49.

52   *Earthly Verses*: The title uses the plural of *āyeh*, which specifically refers to verses of the Quran, divine verses dictated to the Prophet Mohammad by God, not ordinary lines of poetry.

56   *I speak from the limit of night*: Farrokhzad's first three lines repeat the construction "*man az ____ harf mīzanam.*" In Persian *az* can mean either "of" or "from." While an English translator must choose between "I speak *of* ____" or "I speak *from* ____," for the Persian reader both of these possible readings remain simultaneously available.

57   *Green Illusion*: In Persian the word *khīyāl*, suggests an illusion about something concrete, something you could imagine, like a wall or a road or a garden. Here *vahm*, as "illusion," is more abstract, like an instinct, something passing through the mind.

   the stink of my paper crown: From the context of the poem I read this as an allusion to a marriage contract, "a halo of legal legitimacy" made up of the pieces of paper that represent the "crowning achievement" for a woman.

62   *sīmorghs*: The sīmorgh is a mythical, divine bird who lives on the heights of Mount Qaf. See also page 78.

63   *uprising*: The word *rastākhīz* can be read as either Resurrection or Day of Judgment, or as revolt or uprising. *Hezb-e Rastākhīz* was the political party of the Shah at the time.

65 *O Jeweled Land*: This was the title of the national anthem at the time of the Shah.

66 *PLASCO factory*: This was the largest plastic factory in Iran at the time.

Sheikh Abū Clown ... kamāncheh-player ... a tombak in the tanbūr family: Like all the "sophisticated" and "westernized" intellectuals of the time, Farrokhzad is here mocking the Sufi practitioners, their spiritual leaders, the shaikhs, as well as traditional Persian music and musical instruments. The kamāncheh is a traditional stringed instrument played with a bow. The tombak is a traditional hand drum. Before the 1979 Revolution, the stringed tanbūr was reserved for use only at spiritual gatherings.

Navzer watches: A fancy watch brand and a status symbol, as a Rolex might be now.

67 *Zāyandeh river*: The major river running through the city of Esfahān, which was seasonally dry in 1960 but is now, due to water mismanagement, permanently dry.

Grand Ideal Lottery: The proceeds from this national lottery, started by the Shah's sister Princess Ashraf, were supposed to help poor people and fund social services.

a few snorts of first-rate product: Heroin.

"Yā-Haqq" ... "Yā-Hū" ... "Bowwow" ... "Hoo-Hoo": The first two are exclamations Sufis make during zekr, or ritual prayer; the latter two calls of a dog and an owl. All these sounds are meant to ridicule Sufi practice.

school of thug dancing: Enforcers, local thugs who were paid for their "protection" and preyed on local communities. Thugs and intellectuals crossed paths in the back rooms of shops, over heroin and alcohol.

Shams-e Tabrīzī: "*Shams*" means "sun," and so the phrase is both a reference to the year according to the solar calendar and also a mocking reference to the classical poet Rumi, whose teacher was Shams-e Tabrīzī.

OSHNU: The cheapest and worst-smelling Iranian cigarettes at the time.

68   *Majles*: Farrokhzad is mocking the two houses of parliament.

    Bullet Square: Meydān-e Tīr, a barren open ground reserved for military use.

    Execution Square: Meydān-e E'dām, the location of criminal executions during the Qajar dynasty (late 19th century).

    Artillery Square: Meydān-e Tūpkhāneh, a central square in Tehran where criminals were usually hung. See also note to page 95.

69   *Master Teacher Abraham Sabhā*: Ebrāhīm Sahbā was the most famous traditionalist versifier of the time. Farrokhzad's mockery of him is compounded here by her use of the western form of his first name.

71   *dark verse*: *Āyeh*, a verse of the Quran; indelible, of divine origin. See note for page 52.

89   *Book of Kings*: The *Shāhnāmeh*, by classical poet Ferdowsi (late 10th century CE), is the national historical epic of Iran.

    History to End All Histories: The *Nāsekh ol-Tavārīkh* is a multi-volume history of Iran composed by a court historian, Lesān ol-Molk-e Sepehr, during the Qajar dynasty.

90   *Mahdī*: In Shia Islam the Twelfth Imam, the Mahdī, who is hidden, will reveal Himself to establish a just government on Earth. See also page 93.

93   *eyelids keep twitching / and my shoes always land as a pair*: Popular superstition says that if your eyelid twitches, or if when removing your shoes they land together as a pair, someone important is coming to visit.

    Mahdī: See note for page 90.

    owns all rooms in our house: The speaker lives in a tenement building, in which the rooms are leased separately to different tenants.

    The Judge of Judges or He Who Grants Every Need: Two of the divine names of God.

he can take away a thousand from twenty million: In the 1960s it was thought there were a thousand families in Iran that ruled the country of twenty million. The line suggests that one could remove the ruling class without any adverse effect on the rest of the population.

94 *Mohammadyeh Square*: Square in South Tehran that serves working-class neighborhoods.

sleep on the roof: The roofs of Iranian houses are flat—a place for drying clothes, picnicking, and sleeping in hot weather.

Mellī Park: A municipal park in Tehran, now renamed.

Fardīn's movies: Alī Fardīn was a wrestler and popular movie star in pre-Revolutionary Iran.

95 *Tūpkhāneh's sky*: Famous square in downtown Tehran, site of political gatherings and the hanging of criminals. Also known as Artillery Square. See also note to page 68.

Selected Bibliography

My primary text for these translations is *The Complete Collected Poems of Forough Farrokhzad* (مجموعه ی کامل اشعار فروغ فرخزاد) published by Alpha Publishing, an imprint of Wisehouse Publishing, in Sweden in 2017. Sections of the original that were excised by censors I have supplemented with text from other print and online versions.

SELECTED BIOGRAPHICAL AND CRITICAL WORKS

Brookshaw, Dominic Parviz and Nasrin Rahimieh, Eds. *Forough Farrokhzad: Poet of Modern Iran*. London: I. B. Tauris & Co., Ltd., 2010.

Darznik, Jasmin. *Song of a Captive Bird: A Novel*. New York: Random House, 2018. A novel based on the life of Farrokhzad.

Hillmann, Michael C. *A Lonely Woman: Forough Farrokhzad and Her Poetry*. Boulder, Colorado: Lynne Rienner Publishers, Inc., 1987.

Milani, Farzaneh. *Forough Farrokhzad: A Literary Biography with Unpublished Letters*. (فروغ فرخزاد: زندگی نامه ی ادبی همراه با نامه های چاپ نشده) Toronto: Persian Circle Press, 2016.

Milani, Farzaneh. *Veils and Words: The Emerging Voice of Iranian Women Writers*. Syracuse, New York: Syracuse University Press, 1992.

Milani, Farzaneh. *Words, Not Swords: Iranian Women Writers and the Freedom of Movement*. Syracuse, New York: Syracuse University Press, 2011.

SELECTED TRANSLATIONS

Javadi, Hassan, and Susan Sallée. *Forough Farrokhzad: Another Birth and Other Poems*. Washington, DC: Mage Publishers, 2010.

Karimi-Hakkak, Ahmad. *An Anthology of Modern Persian Poetry*. Boulder, Colorado: Westview Press, 1978.

Kessler, Jascha, with Amin Banani. *Bride of Acacias: Selected Poems of Forough Farrokhzad*. Delmar, New York: Caravan Books, 1982.

Martin, David. *A Rebirth*. Costa Mesa, California: Mazda Publishers, 1997.

Sophia, Meetra. *If I Were God: The Writings of Forough Farrokhzad*. San Francisco: City Lights Books, 2008.

Wolpé, Sholeh. *Sin: Selected Poems of Forough Farrokhzad*. Fayetteville, Arkansas: The University of Arkansas Press, 2007.

Acknowledgments

My primary debt is reflected in this book's dedication.

For decades, Iraj Anvar has been my guide, companion, and collaborator in the world of classical and contemporary Persian poetry. A friend of Farrokhzad's brother, Fereydoun, Iraj knew Farrokhzad from her time in Rome, where he was working in avant-garde theater and film. I am grateful not only for his understanding of the language and the literature, and for his patience, but for his generous sharing of his experience of Farrokhzad's milieu in Rome and Tehran.

I am grateful to Farzaneh Milani for suggesting I look more closely at some of the rarely-translated poems in *Osyān*. I have included several poems written during Farrokhzad's stay in Munich.

Thank you, Niloufar Talebi, for your keen eye and wise advice at the end.

I would like to thank the editors of *The Paris Review*, *Poetry International*, *Golden Handcuffs Review*, and *Mantis* for publishing some of these poems, sometimes in slightly different versions.

I would also like to thank Jeffrey Yang, Barbara Epler, Mieke Chew, Erik Rieselbach, and the rest of the team at New Directions for entrusting me with this work, and for seeing it into the world.

I am also grateful to my husband, Chip Loomis, and my sons Sam and William, for welcoming Farrokhzad into our COVID-19 pod for the duration.

Forough Farrokhzad (1934–1967) was born the third of seven children in Mazandaran, north of Tehran. Drawn to reading and writing poetry as a child, she dropped out of high school to study painting and dressmaking at a technical school. At age sixteen she fell in love with her mother's cousin; they married, moved to a provincial town, and had a son. During her marriage, she worked as a seamstress and wrote the poems of her first collection, *The Captive* (1955). In the fall of 1955, she divorced her husband, relinquished all rights to her son, and moved to Tehran. In the fall of 1955, she had a nervous breakdown and underwent electroshock therapy. Three more poetry collections followed: *The Wall* (1956), *Rebellion* (1958), and *Another Birth* (1964). She also translated the work of George Bernard Shaw and Henry Miller; lived in Rome and Germany; returned to Tehran and worked at a literary magazine and at the film studio of Ebrahīm Golestān; studied film production in England; and made a groundbreaking documentary, *The House Is Black* (1962), about a leper colony in northeastern Iran. Her posthumous collection of late poems *Let Us Believe in the Beginning of the Cold Season* was published in 1974.

Elizabeth T. Gray, Jr. is the author of the poetry books *Salient* and *Series | India*, and the translator of *Wine and Prayer: Eighty Ghazals from the Diwan of Hafiz* and *Iran: Poems of Dissent*.

ABOUT UNCLE

Rebecca Gisler

Translated from French
by Jordan Stump

TWO LINES
PRESS

Two Lines Press
582 Market Street, Suite 700, San Francisco, CA 94104
www.twolinespress.com

ISBN 978-1-949641-55-4
Ebook ISBN 978-1-949641-56-1

Cover design by Kapo Ng
Cover art by Nicolas Party, *3 Portraits* (detail), 2017
© Nicolas Party. Courtesy the artist and Hauser & Wirth
Photo: Max C Lee-Russell
Typeset by Stephanie Nisbet

Library of Congress Cataloging-in-Publication Data
Names: Gisler, Rebecca, 1991- author. | Stump, Jordan, 1959- translator.
Title: About uncle / Rebecca Gisler ; translated from French by Jordan Stump.
Other titles: D'oncle. English
Description: San Francisco, CA : Two Lines Press, [2024] | Originally
published as D'oncle in 2021.
Identifiers: LCCN 2023021558 (print) | LCCN 2023021559 (ebook) | ISBN
9781949641554 (paperback) | ISBN 9781949641561 (ebook)
Subjects: LCGFT: Novels.
Classification: LCC PQ2707.I746 D6613 2024 (print) | LCC PQ2707.I746
(ebook) | DDC 843/.92--dc23/eng/20230504
LC record available at https://lccn.loc.gov/2023021558
LC ebook record available at https://lccn.loc.gov/2023021559

1 3 5 7 9 10 8 6 4 2

This book is published with the support of the Swiss Arts Council
Pro Helvetia, and in part by an award from
the National Endowment for the Arts.